Getting Free

Bert Ghezzi

Getting Free

How to Overcome
Persistent Personal Problems

SOPHIA INSTITUTE PRESS®
Manchester, New Hampshire

Getting Free: How to Overcome Persistent Personal Problems was origi-
nally published in 1982 by Servant Books, Ann Arbor, Michigan,
with a different subtitle. This 2001 edition by Sophia Institute Press
includes additions and slight revisions to the original text.

Copyright © 1982; 2001 Bert Ghezzi

Scripture quotations are from the Revised Standard Version of the
Bible, Copyright © 1946, 1952, 1971, 1973, and from the New
American Bible, Copyright © 1970 by the Confraternity of Chris-
tian Doctrine, Washington, D.C.

Printed in the United States of America

Jacket design by Lorraine Bilodeau

Jacket photograph by Peter Griffith, courtesy of Masterfile

Sophia Institute Press®
Box 5284, Manchester, NH 03108
1-800-888-9344
www.sophiainstitute.com

Library of Congress Cataloging-in-Publication Data

Ghezzi, Bert.
    Getting free : how to overcome persistent personal problems /
Bert Ghezzi.
        p.   cm.
    Originally published: Ann Arbor, Mich. : Servant Books, 1982.
    ISBN 1-928832-24-5 (pbk. : alk. paper)
    1. Christian life — Catholic authors. 2. Sin. I. Title.

BX2350.2.G476 2001
248.8′6 — dc21   2001017025

01 02 03 04 05 06 07 10 9 8 7 6 5 4 3 2

❦

Contents

❦

Part One

Recognizing the Problem

v

*

Preface

※

This past week I read *Getting Free* for the first time since I wrote it twenty years ago. As I read, I smiled a little at the confidence and authority I heard in my own voice teaching about overcoming persistent problems. That's because some of my own problems — irritability, anger, and the tendency to be judgmental, to name a few prominent ones — have persisted, and I still have to fight them with all the spiritual energy God gives me. When I put the book down, however, I thought that the ideas in it were still sound and useful.

I say this to caution you that although the strategy I describe here works for overcoming evil influences we find within our hearts, it doesn't always eliminate them.

Unless God intervenes miraculously, some temptations of the flesh stay with us and require us to fight them throughout our lives. So although the strategy presented in *Getting Free* will help you to find release from some big problems, it doesn't offer deliverance from all persistent problems — only a wise, practical way to deal with them and to stay on top of them.

While I updated and slightly revised the text, I decided not to tamper with the examples in the original book, many of which I drew from my family. The children you meet, for example, in the book's opening story, have grown up. As you might suspect, their problems have persisted. The big tease, who appears on page 7, is now a prosecuting attorney, and he still delivers witty but devastating one-liners. I plan to give him and all of my children a copy of this book with the hope that they will read it and apply its teaching in their lives.

You can read *Getting Free* as a how-to book of things you must do to overcome persistent problems. But using it only that way may make matters worse by putting pressure on you to accomplish something humanly impossible. Or you can read it as an opportunity to open yourself up to the marvelous action of the Holy Spirit and let Him accomplish what is divinely possible: setting you free to deal with your problems and conquer them.

Bert Ghezzi
December 2000

*

Getting Free

Part One

✢

Recognizing the Problem

Chapter One

*

*Identify your persistent
personal problems*

My twelve-year-old daughter, Elaine, loves horses. Recently she has been negotiating a trade with me: horseback riding lessons for violin. (She doesn't know it, but my natural reaction against listening to violin exercises is a point in her favor.) Horses are often the subject of conversation in our house. "Ruth's horse," I heard Elaine telling her mother, "is seven-eighths Arabian, I think." Just then her brother passed through the kitchen. Perfectly imitating her tone and cadence, he chirped wickedly, "Elaine is seven-eighths shrimp, I think." My poor wife laughed before she could catch herself.

Teasing of this sort has been a common problem in my family. The young man who delivered the above-quoted line is a master of the art. He seems to be made of the stuff that produces the likes of Bob Hope, those who are famous for dropping negative, although outrageously funny, one-liners. But our stand-up comedian, after many lectures and some parental applause (clapping one flat stick against a child's posterior), has come to regard his teasing as a problem. He has resolved a number of times to stop. Invariably, he has slipped and stung one of us. "I have a problem with teasing, don't I, Dad?" he asked me once. "Well, I try to stop, but I can't. I guess something in me keeps making me do it."

My son is not alone in his plight. Many Christians have problems they think they can't overcome. Sometimes their problems crop up after they've experienced a genuine spiritual renewal. What a terrible irony: to be filled with the Holy Spirit and to be plagued with apparently incurable problems! Is there a Christian who hasn't echoed my son's complaint: "I try to stop but something in me keeps making me do it"?

Most people have some emotional difficulties such as anger, self-condemnation, unruly desires, or fears. Many have faults or weaknesses that must change. All are sinners. Consider the following real-life examples.

⋇

Anger and anxiety may trouble us
Tom and Sally, both active members of their parish, were married two years ago. As single people, they had

been regarded as model young Christian adults. None-theless, these fine young people had a very difficult time adjusting to married life. Major changes in a person's life, such as marriage, often flush out problems that have been hidden below the surface.

Sally, who had been very active in parish groups, felt that Tom's desire for her to spend more time at home was selfish. It deprived her of her ministry. In addition, Tom's tendency to make snap decisions and his con-stant, low-level irritability made Sally fearful for their future relationship. It didn't take long before her wor-ries swelled into full-fledged anxiety.

Tom had always been a little capricious. He had a long-standing problem with irritability. He interpreted Sally's difficulty with his impulsive decision-making as unwarranted criticism. He felt pressured by her resis-tance to his desire for her to stay at home more. As a re-sult, his irritability grew worse until it sparked frequent arguments between them.

Tom and Sally knew they had problems. They both tried to stop. Neither could. Something seemed to pre-vent them from changing.

Tom's irritability and Sally's anxiety are examples of emotional problems. Modern Christians seem to have more problems with their emotions than Christians of earlier — say, for example, New Testament — times. Our functionalized society compels us to place a very high value on intimacy, and feelings are among our most intimate parts. Our whole environment prepares us to pay keen attention to how we feel. But the more attention we pay to our emotions, the more problems we find or make for ourselves.

Don't misunderstand. As Christians, we shouldn't model ourselves on stoics, striving to be free from our feelings. Instead, we should model ourselves on Jesus and His disciples. We should try to do everything *with* feeling: get angry, cry at funerals, leap for joy. But the modern tendency to overemphasize feelings creates a host of problems for us.

༈

Addictions can enslave us

Most of us know someone who has struggled to be free of alcohol or drug addiction. Another, more subtle addiction, and one that afflicts contemporary Christians, is the TV habit.

Jack, an insurance salesman, father of three, and faithful usher at his local parish, is one such TV addict.

In the past year he has developed the habit of turning on the TV whenever his wife is upstairs nursing the baby. At times, he has become hooked by some utterly mindless show, spending up to two hours hypnotized by the electronic box. His wife has begun to miss the few private times they had together. But Jack doesn't seem able to divorce himself from his new pastime.

Jack's TV habit may seem harmless enough. But in reality it is the kind of attachment that may lead to idolatry. Habitual dependency on the media, food, sex, or anything else usually involves a degree of devotion that is improper. What seems innocent may, at its root, border on serious wrongdoing. In Jack's case, his seemingly harmless addiction may soon result in broken relationships with his wife and family.

⚹

Curiosity can become sinful

Mary works as a receptionist for the local county social-service office for family counseling. Her job gives her access to confidential files that detail cases being reviewed by the bureau's counselors. Mary needs to handle the files, but rarely does any assignment require her to delve into them. But delve into them she does.

Ever since she was a child, Mary has been very curious about the personal lives of others. She has been reading other people's letters since she was about fifteen years old. Now she feels an inner drive to explore the files at work. The more she indulges the desire, the more it seems to grow. Mary is a Catholic who takes her Faith to heart, but curiosity is a big problem for her. She has sought the advice of her pastor, but, as yet, she has not overcome her problem.

Mary's curiosity is a disorderly desire. It may have its root in some serious sin, such as envy or pride. And it may lead to serious wrongdoing, such as deceit (covering her tracks) or slander (telling others what she has discovered). Inability to control such tendencies is a fairly typical problem for Christians.

⚜

Impure thoughts can lead to sinful behavior

Mark is the art director for an advertising agency. He and his wife, Anne, lead part of their parish's marriage-enrichment program. The periodicals Mark must consult for his artwork for his job often contain suggestive photos, and he knows he lingers over them. Now and then, on business trips, he even indulges his desire to spend an evening alone in his motel room reading a pornographic magazine. For several years now, his mind has been full of sexual fantasies.

Mark occasionally rationalizes his behavior to himself, pretending that his mental promiscuity enhances his sexual relationship with Anne. But when he considers it objectively, he admits this isn't true. Moreover, since his meditations frequently result in masturbation, he has not persuaded himself that the fantasies are permissible. Mark thinks he has a problem that he'll never get rid of.

Sexual desire in itself is not a problem. This desire is the Creator's gift, planted in us to bind us to His purposes for humanity. Sexual desire is good. Nor are sexual temptations (even the most explicitly pornographic ones) exactly problems, unless we let them take control. Sexual temptations, like any temptation, are desires to do something God has outlawed. They might be difficult to resist, and we might call the struggle a problem, but the sexual temptation itself is not the problem — our response is.

When do sexual thoughts become sin? A priest once asked a young man in the confessional, "Have you been entertaining any impure thoughts lately?" The young man responded, "Oh no, Father, but they sure have been entertaining me!" Sexual thoughts are wrong only if we indulge them, letting them entertain us with vicarious sexual pleasures. Every Christian must handle sexual desires. For many, at one time or another, they become the beginning of a problem.

⚜

Believe that we can get free of our problems

In several places, the New Testament lists serious problems that stem from the flesh. If we aren't impressed by these lists, we should be. They're directed not to pagans, but to Christians. The Lord knew that His children would be tempted to sin, so He warned us in advance:

> Now the works of the flesh are plain: fornication, impurity, licentiousness, idolatry, sorcery, enmity, strife, jealousy, anger, selfishness, dissension, party spirit, envy, drunkenness, carousing, and the like. I warn you, as I warned you before, that those who do such things shall not inherit the kingdom of God.[1]

[1] Gal. 5:19-21.

The Bible presents such lists not to crush us, but to put us on the alert. We often feel trapped by our problems, but the Lord wants us to know that help is at hand.

The list of problems contemporary Christians face — including addiction, boredom, criticalness, depression, materialism, gossip, negativity, presumption, worry, and unreliability — is extensive. If you recognize problems in your own life, don't be disheartened. All of us tend to feel bad about ourselves when we fail, but grief for wrongdoing is good only if it's based on having offended God. Then we can turn away from our old behavior. Grief for grief's sake is itself an offense. Only repentance that leads to change pleases God.

Have you tried to change but failed? Are you like my son who cannot stop teasing: "Something in me keeps making me do it"? If you have problems that won't go away, the Lord has help for you. The Church through Scripture, teaching, and the sacraments presents a way of getting free from such problems.

This book aims to set forth that strategy in very practical terms. In the next chapter we will discuss the most common approach that Christians take to problems, one that never works.

Chapter Two

❧

Don't rely on
willpower alone

＊

"Scripture says that God helps those who help themselves," declared the older of two men, whose animated discussion was verging on argument. He hoped to support his point by appealing to authority. Some onlookers were embarrassed for the man. Others found themselves stifling smiles. Everyone except the speaker seemed to know that this line appears nowhere in the Bible.

Seldom are serious Christians fooled by this bogus Bible verse. They instinctively recognize it as a worldly notion masquerading as spiritual wisdom. They see that it bends people away from God, who saves us, toward self, which can't save anyone. Yet, judging by our daily behavior, I'd have to conclude that many serious Christians conduct their lives as if "God helps those who help themselves" were a cardinal, biblical directive.

Willpower Christianity is perhaps the most common approach to living the Christian life. Men and women come to know the Lord and experience His love for them in a personal way. They hear and understand His teaching, His commands, and His principles, and they eagerly embrace them. But they make a big mistake when they begin to apply them to their own lives. They engage their wills as the chief, if not sole, agent charged with getting their lives in order.

Consider again the examples cited in the first chapter. The men and women presented in these vignettes are serious about their Christianity. Some were born and raised in Catholic families and later made an adult commitment to Christ. For example, Mary, who struggles with curiosity, can't remember a time when she didn't feel drawn to the Lord. She recalls with joy the high school retreat at which she openly committed herself to follow Him and how excited she was when she received the sacrament of Confirmation. Others, such as Tom and Sally, came to know the Lord as adults and have dedicated themselves to serving Him. All of them want to please the Lord and live their lives in accord with His teaching. Each of them, however, seems to have adopted the willpower approach.

It must be said that some of them have had a limited measure of success with it. Hearing and understanding

God, deciding to do what He wants, and charging the will to accomplish it can be somewhat effective. When Mark, the art director, heard at a parish mission that Christians should pray regularly, he decided the following Monday to begin a daily morning prayer time, which he has been faithful to ever since. His wife, Anne, once heard a homily on hospitality, saw what generosity the Lord expects of us toward guests, and decided to set aside the reluctance she had had toward opening her home to others. Deciding was enough, for ever since, Anne and Mark have graciously hosted a fairly continuous stream of guests.

But Mark and Anne, Tom and Sally, Mary and the others got only so far with willpower Christianity. A simple decision seemed to bring some areas right into line with the Lord's design for them. But when their wills encountered resistance, they were stymied and failed to enact the decision. On what must seem to him to be innumerable occasions, Tom has decided to stop being irritable, but he has not been able to obey his own commands. Something resists. Mark is discouraged and sometimes ashamed of the inability of his willpower to keep him from indulging in sexual fantasies. Something resists.

Thus, willpower Christianity, as popular as it is, has only limited effectiveness. Some things our will can push right into place. Others it can't budge, no matter how hard we try.

In his letter to the Romans, Paul describes from his own experience the plight of the Christian who takes the willpower approach:

> I do not understand my own actions. For I do not do what I want, but I do the very thing I hate. Now if I do what I do not want, I agree that the law is good. So then it is no longer I that do it, but sin which dwells within me. For I know that nothing good dwells within me, that is, in my flesh. I can will what is right, but I cannot do it. For I do not do the good I want, but the evil I do not want is what I do. . . . So I find it to be a law that when I want to do right, evil lies close at hand. For I delight in the law of God, in my inmost self, but I see in my members another law at war with the law of my mind and making me captive to the law of sin which dwells in my members.[2]

[2] Rom. 7:15-19, 21-23.

Every Christian can identify with the struggle depicted in this passage. At one time or another we all attempt to accomplish by willpower what we could have freely received from the Lord by living the life of the Spirit.

> For the law of the Spirit of life in Christ Jesus has set me free from the law of sin and death. For God has done what the law, weakened by the flesh, could not do.[3]

Alone we can't apply the law to our life. Sheer willpower isn't enough. When we understand God's requirements and try to obey, we discover there is more going on than the activity of our intellect and will. We encounter external obstacles. We find resistance within. We shouldn't be surprised to find it, for that resistance is inextricably bound up with ourselves.

Walt Kelly's cartoon character Pogo Possum used to say, "We have met the enemy, and he is us." In his contrast of life in the Spirit and life under the law, this is the reality Paul describes as "the law, weakened by the flesh." Willpower Christianity, or the law approach, is

[3] Rom. 8:2-3.

not enough, because it expects an individual human to overcome a set of obstacles that no mere human could ever expect to master. This is a hard saying to accept in the contemporary age, when self-reliance has become, even among Christians who should know better, the virtue par excellence. Self-reliance is good, but it's no match for the hostility hurled at us by our enemy.

Chapter Three

⚹

Know what you're up against

The law approach to Christian living, although it can't bring us into perfect conformity with the ways of God nor deliver us from all of our problems, has this particular advantage: it can demonstrate that we're up against an enemy larger than ourselves and that, whatever it is, we can't handle it on our own. Learning this truth is a valuable lesson. It's even worth a few bouts with self-reliance, if we learn it well.

Problems that I encounter in my Christian life may lead to either doom or deliverance. They lead to doom if I am overcome by them and succumb. But problems can lead to deliverance if I approach them properly. Every obstacle I encounter living as a Christian can be both an opportunity for grace and a chance for me to acquire more wisdom about the enemy's operations.

Obstacles to Christian living stem from a complex of interrelated sources. None of them will submit to taming by mere human authority. Scripture describes them as mighty spiritual forces linked in a determined conspiracy to destroy humanity. Their traditional names are the world, the flesh, and the Devil.

Under the influence of modern styles of thought, some Catholics have carelessly lost a healthy sense of fear in the face of these deadly foes. We should not spurn the benefits of human wisdom, but at the same time we dare not let current intellectual fashions blind us to the spiritual realities that God says will harm us if we don't stay alert. What better way to destroy us than to persuade us that sin, the world, the flesh, and the Devil are merely metaphysical byproducts of the primitive cultures in which Scripture was written, and certainly not real or dangerous? We might thus be lulled into surrender without putting up a fight.

※

The world leads us away from God

The world, as defined in Scripture, is an inhospitable place for humanity. Scripture declares that the world is opposed to the Father and that friendship with the world makes a person an enemy of God. "Do not love the world," wrote John, "or the things in the world. If anyone loves the world, love for the Father is not in him. For all that is in the world, the lust of the flesh and the lust of the eyes and the pride of life, is not of the Father but is of the world."[4] James is even more pointed: "Do you not know that friendship with the world is enmity with God? Therefore whoever wishes to be a friend of the world makes himself an enemy of God."[5]

These are hard words indeed for many contemporary Catholics. Some balk at the notion that the world is an enemy, because they mistakenly think that the term refers to all of creation. But the same Creator who warns us about the world has declared that all that He made is good.[6] The created world, then, isn't the enemy.

Some Christians, out of love for humanity, dedicate themselves in generous service to improving human conditions, but in the process grow somewhat contemptuous of the idea that the world is our enemy. These Christians would do well to recover the traditional wariness of the world. Otherwise they may find themselves serving under enemy banners. They are in danger

[4] 1 John 2:15-16.
[5] James 4:4.
[6] See Gen. 1.

of becoming infatuated with a gospel whose primary agenda has become a secularized one.

The world, in the biblical warnings cited, doesn't re-fer to creation or the natural realm; nor does it simply indicate the affairs of humanity, human achievements, or humanitarianism. The world that is inimical to man is unredeemed human society, the aggregate of men and women who don't serve the Lord. The world consists of the relationships, practices, policies, and plans of the millions who remain in bondage to the empire of dark-ness, sin, and death. It isn't a safe place for Christians to walk unawares. It's an environment that bends us away from God. We pick up its ways unconsciously, through imitation, social influence, education, and the media.

For example, polls and studies indicate that many Catholics and other Christians immersed in our con-temporary secular environment conduct themselves no differently from non-Christians in matters such as abor-tion and extramarital sex. Their behavior and opinions seem to be influenced more by peer pressure and the evening news than by the gospel of Christ or by the Church. They are like pedestrians walking on the next block when a parade passes by: without even knowing it, they walk to the cadence of the drums.

The world is a significant source of the personal problems that many Catholics experience. The conditions of our society are ideal for fostering emotional difficulties. The prevailing tone of conversation is often negative and critical. People seldom encourage one another, and they express little or no affection. At work and in groups, we have to watch out for people who might use us or climb over us to reach their goals. These patterns are the basic material from which problems with fear, insecurity, low self-esteem, and anxiety are woven.

❧

Sin weakens our efforts to be good

The force at work in the world that turns us away from the Lord is sin. I do not mean sin simply as individual acts of wrongdoing, but sin as an objective, powerful force.

Notice that this is the meaning of sin that Paul talks about in his letter to the Romans:

What then shall we say? That the law is sin? By no means! Yet, if it had not been for the law, I should not have known sin. I should not have known what it is to covet if the law had not said,

"You shall not covet." But sin, finding opportunity in the commandment, wrought in me all kinds of covetousness. Apart from the law sin lies dead. I was once alive apart from the law, but when the commandment came, sin revived and I died; the very commandment which promised life proved to be death to me. For sin, finding opportunity in the commandment, deceived me and by it killed me.[7]

Sin here is not merely a particular act of covetousness. Nor is it merely the aggregation of many acts of wrongdoing. Paul regards sin as an objective condition. Sin is a reality that operates on us. It takes advantage of the commandments, using them to destroy us. In this particular case, sin, which Paul speaks of as a spiritual substance, works on us like one of the Sirens in Greek mythology, luring us by enchanted song onto the rocks of wrongdoing and, ultimately, to death.

Sin sums up in itself the alienation of unredeemed humanity from God. Thus, it constitutes a constant state of war: creature versus Creator. This explains why

[7] Rom. 7:7-11.

mere human effort — willpower Christianity on any scale — can't ultimately solve the problems we face. When a veteran baseball player replaces the rookie who has committed three errors and then makes the game-losing error himself, his teammates complain that the rookie had so messed up left field that no one could have played it. The same sort of situation exists on a grander scale in the world. Sin has messed things up so much that we can't straighten them out by our own power.

⚹

The Devil tries to deceive us into sinning

We are not up against some accidental dislocation of our relationship with the Lord. The way sin operates in the world isn't haphazard. Scripture says that Satan, the self-declared enemy of God and man, masterminds the effort against God's work on the earth. "Your adversary the Devil," warns Peter, "prowls around like a roaring lion, seeking someone to devour."[8] Paul addresses the Ephesians, saying, "You were dead through the trespasses and sins in which you once walked, following the

---

[8] 1 Pet. 5:8.

course of this world, following the prince of the power of the air, the spirit that is now at work in the sons of disobedience. Among these we all once lived in the passions of our flesh, following the desires of body and mind, and so we were by nature children of wrath, like the rest of mankind."[9] John puts it succinctly: "We know that we are of God, and the whole world is in the power of the evil one."[10]

If we have carelessly allowed this personal enemy to fade into some vague fog of impersonal evil forces, we should correct our mistake.

The New Testament shows that Jesus' spiritual warfare wasn't a case of good versus evil, impersonal forces at war with one another, but God versus Satan. From the beginning of His ministry, Jesus exercised His Father's authority over personal evil spirits, calling demons by name and casting them out. In the end, Jesus, the sinless Victim, conquered death, stripping power from Satan, His personal enemy.

The contemporary reduction of the Devil to a legend is a clever ploy. What better way for the Devil to

[9] Eph. 2:1-3.
[10] 1 John 5:19.

catch humans off guard than to evaporate into the thin air of a theological discussion?

Satan is the architect of an empire of grand design he has erected in opposition to the kingdom of God on the earth. He has assembled a vast army of his servants, both spiritual and human, and deployed them in manifold ways to achieve his purposes. He masterminds their influence on people throughout the earth. He and his hosts of fallen angels craftily spin webs of deceit to ensnare hapless humans, whom they hope to destroy. Temptations that shimmer with allurement and lies that seem to have the ring of truth are among his most effective weapons. Confusion, doubt, and anxiety are deadly arrows in his quiver.

Satan, the would-be mastermind of our doom, is an enemy not to be trifled with. No one, on his own strength or will, except Jesus Christ Himself, is any match for him.

The Cross of Jesus Christ has assured Satan of his final defeat. Still, he lingers on, attempting by whatever means to take with him into that defeat as many humans as he can. Like a great spider, he would sting us into submission so that he might devour us at will. This in fact is the enemy's specific purpose for us. After the final summing up of human history, which Christians expect at the Second Coming, the Devil will feed eternally on those people foolish enough to follow him.

⚜

External forces aren't our only problems

The world, sin, and the Devil have thrown uncountable, miserable obstacles in our paths. But before we blame them entirely for our problems, we must admit that something in us is inclined to collaborate with the enemy.

Chapter Four

*Be vigilant against
the flesh*

We have formidable external enemies. The problems Christians face daily are largely traceable to the activities of these enemies. But we must admit that a considerable part of our problem comes from within ourselves. The world, sin, and the Devil tantalize us into doing things we hate; they prevent us from obeying God's law and from molding our life according to His principles.

But our experience tells us that something inside us collaborates with our enemies. Something within us opposes our desire to follow the Lord. We usually know what is right, and we generally hate what is wrong. What is it that makes us do the very things we hate? The word that some translations of Scripture use to name this something is *the flesh*.

For those who live according to the flesh set their minds on the things of the flesh, but those who live according to the Spirit set their minds on the things of the Spirit. To set the mind on the flesh is death, but to set the mind on the Spirit is life and peace. For the mind that is set on the flesh is hostile to God; it does not submit to God's law, indeed it cannot; and those who are in the flesh cannot please God. But you are not in the flesh, you are in the Spirit, if in fact the Spirit of God dwells in you.[11]

For you were called to freedom, brethren; only do not use your freedom as an opportunity for the flesh, but through love be servants of one another. . . . But I say, walk by the Spirit, and do not gratify the desires of the flesh. For the desires of the flesh are against the Spirit, and the desires of the Spirit are against the flesh; for these are opposed to each other, to prevent you from doing what you would.[12]

But I, brethren, could not address you as spiritual men, but as men of the flesh, as babes in Christ. I

[11]Rom. 8:5-9.
[12]Gal. 5:13, 16-17.

fed you with milk, not with solid food; for you were not ready for it; and even yet you are not ready, for you are still of the flesh. For while there is jealousy and strife among you, are you not of the flesh, and behaving like ordinary men?[13]

⚜

"The flesh" is not merely the body, sexual desire, or emotions

In each of these passages, the word *flesh* is used to name that element in us which prevents us from obeying God's law or involves us in some wrongdoing against others.

When the New Testament names that within us which resists God's law, it uses the Greek word transliterated *sarx*. The literal meaning of *sarx* is "body," and sometimes the Bible uses the word in this sense.

Also, in some translations the word *flesh* is used to refer simply to the human body. However, when the New Testament talks about our inner susceptibility to sin and terms it *the flesh*, we should understand that it

[13] 1 Cor. 3:1-3.

isn't talking about our physical body. The New Testament teaches that the flesh — not the body — leads us to sin.

That the flesh operates in our intellect confirms this fact. Paul's letter to the Galatians catalogs the works of the flesh: immorality, impurity, licentiousness, idolatry, sorcery, enmity, strife, jealousy, anger, selfishness, dissension, party spirit, envy, drunkenness, and carousing.[14] All of these, including those with an emotional or sexual component, are based in our mind. Jesus Himself taught that "what comes out of the mouth proceeds from the heart, and this defiles a man. For out of the heart come evil thoughts, murder, adultery, fornication, theft, false witness, slander."[15] It isn't the physical body that tempts us to such wrongdoing, but the flesh, working in our thoughts and desires.

Christians frequently confuse the flesh with sexuality. However, when the New Testament teaches about the flesh, it doesn't equate it with sexual desire. This isn't to say that the flesh doesn't seduce us into sexual sin. It can work to distort our sexuality, but the flesh

[14]Gal. 5:19-21.
[15]Matt. 15:18-19.

isn't itself identical with sexual desire. Sex can work properly in the Christian life, but the "flesh" that Paul speaks of never can.

The Lord gave men and women sexual desire so that they could cooperate with Him in establishing new families as building blocks in the new humanity. Used within the bounds the Lord set for it, sexuality leads not to sin but to good. By exercising vigilance and wisdom, Christians can prevent the flesh from manipulating them into sexual expressions unacceptable to the Lord.

The New Testament does not equate the flesh with our emotions, either. This is an easy mistake for Christians to make in a culture in which the focus on feelings has expanded exponentially. Even though the flesh is distinct from emotions, however, it may play a big part in a person's emotional difficulties. In the case studies presented in the first chapter, Tom's irritability, Sally's anxiety, and Mary's curiosity all constitute emotional problems that have been strongly influenced by the work of the flesh.

If the flesh isn't the body, sexual desire, or the emotions, what is this thing within us that makes us so susceptible to sin?

⚜

The flesh brings us under the influence
of external enemies

Let me borrow an analogy from modern warfare to help us understand the nature of the flesh. At the very end of the Spanish Civil War — a prelude to World War II — the city of Madrid was the last stronghold of loyalist republican forces, who opposed General Franco's armies. Four columns of troops marched against the beleaguered city, and Franco's forces prevailed. According to journalists who reported on the battle, Franco's conquest was assured by the existence of a fifth column inside the city walls, which worked to lay it open to the approaching enemy.

Fifth column has come to mean an enemy within that collaborates with external enemies. The fifth column makes contact with the advancing enemy, takes up its cause within the city, throws the gates open to attack, and aids in the assault that produces defeat.

The New Testament describes the flesh as a fifth column operating within us to bring us under the influence of our external enemies. Sin is at work in the world around us, an enemy out to conquer us. We would be much less vulnerable to its advances were it not that the flesh works on us from within, making contact with sin. The flesh takes up sin's cause by persuading us that it is attractive, even irresistible. The flesh throws open our defenses and escorts the enemy inside.

This enemy within connects with the enemy without. The fruit of their union is an act of wrongdoing or a problem that can correctly be called a work of the flesh.

In Tolkien's *The Two Towers*, King Theoden and his entire kingdom have been reduced to near impotence by the influence of Wormtongue, a traitorous advisor in the service of an enemy. This enemy within has eroded the courage and hope of the aging king and nearly persuaded him to turn away the aid and counsel that comes through the wizard Gandalf and his companions.

When we set our mind on the flesh, it provides the same kind of direction for us as Wormtongue provided for Theoden. The flesh opposes aid and counsel, grace and teaching from God. "For the desires of the flesh are against the Spirit, and the desires of the Spirit are against the flesh; for these are opposed to each other, to prevent you from doing what you would."[16]

[16]Gal. 5:17.

⚜

We must discard the "old man"

The flesh can also be understood as a collection of evil tendencies at work within us. These wicked inclinations are the heritage we have from the "old man." Paul uses this term to refer to our participation in the unredeemed nature of fallen man. We all recognize the old man by his bent: he is turned away from God; he is inclined to evil, and evil is inclined to him; he is always ready for some mischief, never tiring, never satisfied. Weak in the face of sin's allurements, he is strong, even stubborn, when it comes to resisting correction. *Service* and *obedience* are words beyond his comprehension. His one goal in life is self-fulfillment. That's a word the old man understands.

Paul tells the Colossians that they have "put off the old nature with its practices and have put on the new nature, which is being renewed in knowledge after the image of its Creator."[17] Literally, Paul says that they have put off the old man and put on the new man. But traces of the old man must have remained alive and active in the Colossians, since, in this same passage, Paul

[17]Col. 3:9-10.

commands them to put a stop to sins of the flesh: immorality, impurity, anger, malice, slander, and foul talk.

The old man is persistent. Even when we have put him off and put on Christ, the old man's evil tendencies continue to influence us. He hangs around, and we must keep putting him off again and putting on Christ. Paul directs the Ephesians to put off the old man and put on the new man, even though they had been Christians long enough to have expected their old man to be thoroughly dead. "Put off your old nature [man] which belongs to your former manner of life and is corrupt through deceitful lusts, and be renewed in the spirit of your minds, and put on the new nature [man], created after the likeness of God in true righteousness and holiness."[18] The flesh is the residue of the old man in us. He lingers on, to cause us problems — if we let him.

[18]Eph. 4:22-23.

Part Two

✻

Overcoming the Problem

Chapter Five

Let the Lord free you from evil influences

✳

With so great a swarm of enemies threatening us, it is no wonder that we say, "Amen" to the exasperated plea of the Christian in Romans: "Wretched man that I am! Who will deliver me from this body of death?"[19] Mercifully, Paul does not allow the question to go unanswered: "Thanks be to God through Jesus Christ our Lord!"[20]

Paul doesn't present the human condition depicted in Chapter 7 of Romans as an incurable, terminal disease. The Lord, who delivered us from the bondage of sin and death, will also save us in our life. He has already intervened mightily by sending Jesus to alter the once-fatal destiny of humans. He continues to intervene, defending us against our external enemies and freeing us from the treason of the enemy within.

[19]Rom. 7:24.
[20]Rom. 7:25.

⚹

Christ defeated sin and established
a new humanity

God's original plan in creation was to have sons and daughters fashioned in His own image and likeness. They were to know Him, love Him, and live in close communion with Him, sharing His own life. Tempted by Satan, the Lord's personal enemy, they traded the freedom of this union for enslavement to the empire of darkness. In place of eternal life, Satan gave them death. In place of holiness, he gave them sin. Their constant hunger for God, a hunger they had been born with, could never be satisfied. Rather, they found themselves in the service of a counterfeit god whose intent was to devour them.

In spite of their treasonable behavior, the Lord maintained His determination to have a race of men and women in His own image and likeness. He sent the Second Person of the Godhead, His only Son, Jesus Christ, to establish a new humanity. God Himself became a man, embodying the human condition, weakness and all, except for sin. While Jesus lived on earth, He assembled a community of men and women who would be the first to become part of the new humanity. And He waged war against Satan and his armies.

The climactic act of His earthly ministry conquered the enemy and founded the new humanity. The Sinless One took all sin upon Himself and freely submitted to death by crucifixion. But to his shock, Satan could not hold the Lord in death. For Jesus had no sin, and sin was the enemy's only hold on mankind. Thus Jesus defeated the ancient enemy. He broke open the gates of darkness and despoiled Hell of its captives. They became in that moment the Heavenward side of the new human race.

The Holy Spirit breathed new life into Jesus, and He burst from the grave. The New Man returned to His Father's side. From there He poured out on His followers the same Spirit who raised Him from the grave. They were the new humanity on earth, now charged with incorporating all men and women into their communion.

The work of Christ was twofold. By His death and Resurrection, He conquered Satan, sin, and death — man's mortal enemies. He also became the second Adam, the head and founder of a new humanity, the Church.

⚜

The sacraments strengthen and heal us
In God's design, the Church was to spread throughout the earth and throughout the centuries, drawing all

people to Him. To make this possible, He created the sacraments. The sacraments make Christ's saving work available in every time and place, so men and women can become incorporated into the new humanity.

Jesus instituted the sacraments, and guided by the Holy Spirit, the Church has refined and developed them. Today we celebrate seven sacraments: Baptism, Confirmation, and the Eucharist, the sacraments of initiation; Reconciliation and Anointing of the Sick, the sacraments of healing; and Matrimony and Holy Orders, the sacraments of service and mission.

The sacraments of initiation introduce us into the new humanity and sustain us as sons and daughters of God. In the waters of Baptism we enter into Christ's death, shedding the old man, and rise with Christ, putting on the new man. Anointed with oil in Confirmation, we receive divine strength for our daily work of serving God and waging spiritual warfare. When we receive the Body and Blood of Christ in the Eucharist, we renew our participation in the new covenant that created the new humanity. Frequent reception of the Eucharist equips us to live in Christian freedom.

The Lord gave us the sacraments of healing to repair our physical, spiritual, and moral brokenness. Physical and spiritual healing comes to the seriously ill through the Anointing of the Sick. The sacrament of Reconciliation, or Confession, restores our union with God and our full participation in the new humanity, which our wrongdoing damages. Regular Confession provides us with opportunities to receive the Lord's help in dealing with persistent problems caused by the flesh.

Two sacraments prepare us for our mission and service in the Church: Matrimony, for binding a man and woman in mutual love and raising a family; and Holy Orders, to ordain a man to celebrate and administer the sacraments, lead worship, and exercise pastoral leadership in the new humanity.

In a wonderful and mysterious way, each of the sacraments brings us a fresh outpouring of the Holy Spirit, whom, as the culminating act of his ministry, Christ sent to establish and empower the Church. The Holy Spirit works in each of us to free us from our bondage to the flesh.

❧

The Holy Spirit frees us from the grip of the flesh
The Holy Spirit is the presence of God dwelling in the members of the new humanity. He draws Christian

men and women into the very life of the Trinity. His presence within them makes them holy, just as His presence made holy the Temple of Israel. By His manifold gifts, the Holy Spirit equips men and women to build the Christian community according to the mind of God. He is the source of the power that animates and strengthens the followers of Christ for their service. His actions make Christians more like God. He transforms the members of the new humanity so that they grow more perfectly into the image and likeness of the New Man. However, before they can be imprinted with the character of Christ, His followers must be free from the enemy within.

The Spirit delivers Christians from the flesh and its effects by leading them to surrender to Christ and by providing them with an alternative principle for living. Loosed from the fleshly influences that bend them away from God, Christians are free to live in obedience to the Lord. As they do, day by day, their character becomes more like God's — marked by love, joy, peace, patience, kindness, goodness, reliability, generosity, self-control, and the like.[21] So the Holy Spirit empowers the new

[21]See Gal. 5:22-23.

humanity with new life and produces the *character* of the New Man, Jesus Christ, in His brothers and sisters.

⚜

We must open ourselves to the Spirit's power

Release from our enemies is the result of the work of Christ and of the Holy Spirit. Jesus frees us from Satan, sin, and death. The Holy Spirit frees us from the grip of the flesh and its effects on us. Jesus and the Holy Spirit have conquered for us, but if we refuse their power and renounce their methods, we place ourselves in jeopardy. If we insist on self-reliance, on our own strength and strategies, our foes can still do us real harm. We must *appropriate* our Christian freedom. Otherwise, despite victories and broken chains, we will behave like men and women in bondage. To maintain Christ's conquest of Satan and his kingdom, we must master the Lord's strategy and tactics and become adept at using the weapons He gave us. In short, we must wage spiritual warfare.

⚜

The Church teaches us how to live

The Lord established the new humanity itself as the chief antidote to the world and sin. The Church is an alternative environment to that of the world, which is hostile to God and bends His people away from Him.

It stands against the world for the world's own sake. The Church is against the world in obedience to the Lord's direction that we must not love the world, since those who love the world place themselves at enmity with the Father. Practically speaking, Catholics implement this directive by patterning their everyday lives on the teachings of the Church and Scripture.

⚜

Christians should draw others to Christ

So the new humanity must build a Christian subculture, radically different from the dominant culture of the world. Within that subculture, men and women can become what the Lord intends them to be. If we fail to be "against the world," if we build no alternative Christian culture, men and women of God will walk, talk, think, act, live, and die, not in God's ways, but in the ways of those who do not follow Him.

The Church is "for the world" because the Lord loves the men and women who are living in the world. He wants to incorporate them into the new humanity. To be "for the world," our parishes and groups should be characterized by openness and growth. They should be hospitable places that welcome and involve newcomers cheerfully and warmly. The Lord has charged Christians to be His messengers of rescue to the world. *Evangelism*, not *judgment*, must be our watchword. The Church must be busy introducing people to the Lord and to the community of redeemed men and women.

❧

Authority and truth are our spiritual weapons

In the warfare against Satan, the Lord has personally won the decisive battle. He has pulled the lion's teeth, but, for a time, the beast still has claws. The war is won, but will not be over until Jesus comes again to complete human history. In the time remaining to the enemy, which grows shorter with each moment, he works his own evangelism program to ensnare humans with temptations and lies. Between Christ's victory over Satan and the end of time, our warfare is akin to a "mop-up" operation, applying the consequences of defeat to a beaten enemy who has not yet stopped fighting. Authority and the truth are our main weapons, and we should wield them daily.

By the Cross, the Lord has brought Satan under His authority. That same authority is our heritage, because we are sons and daughters of God. Satan roams about behaving as though no one had authority over him. When we fail to exercise our authority as Christians, we allow him to get away with it. Taking authority over the enemy may simply mean commanding him to cease a particular effort he is directing against us or someone for whom we are responsible. Or it may mean taking determined steps to shut out his influence.

For example, we may need to avoid places or people who weaken our resistance to Satan's temptations. To fight temptation is to exercise our divinely appointed authority. This perspective adds a pleasant twist to the grueling business of resisting temptation. Taking authority allows us the pleasure of subduing the enemy, instead of being subdued by him.

Chastened by his defeat at the Cross and restrained by the hand of God from using more dangerous methods, Satan now uses lies as his main weapon. While he awaits the final, inevitable humbling, his only chance to trick us into joining him is by lying. He lies to us about God's love, our salvation, our personal security in Christ, and our status as children of God. He lies about our spouse's fidelity, our friend's loyalty, and our child's obedience. He tempts us to act wrongly and tries to convince us that we have no strength to resist. When Jesus was tempted by Satan's lies, He came through the test by repeating simple, confident statements of the truth.[22] Knowing the truth and holding ourselves to it is our best defense against the Devil.

Our authority in Jesus and our conviction of God's truth will win the day for us as we battle the enemy outside the walls. Now we must turn our attention to release from the enemy within. Sin works in us through the collaboration of our flesh. Overcoming the flesh and the problems it causes is mainly the work of the Holy Spirit in us. Our release from this enemy comes when we learn to surrender our lives fully to Christ and yield ourselves to the power of his Holy Spirit. How to go about this is the subject of the remaining chapters.

[22]Cf. Matt. 4:1-11.

Chapter Six

 ✤

Surrender your problems
to the Holy Spirit

If we expect our problems to disappear by some magic, we are profoundly mistaken. Becoming a Christian normally means having to deal with more problems rather than fewer. We do not experience our patterns of sinful behavior as problems until we know we must get rid of them. Becoming alive to the work of the Holy Spirit can bring to light problems that have long been hidden. When clear, fresh water is poured into a soiled bucket, all the dirt is flushed to the surface. The same is true of the Christian's life. But instead of greeting the situation with dismay, we should be glad for the chance to clean up the mess.

As we have seen, our problems in the Christian life are rooted in the activities of our foes. The Lord's solution for us was radical. By the work of Christ and the work of the Holy Spirit, He has released us from the hold of Satan, the world, sin, and the flesh. Through our commitment to the Lord and our baptism into Him, we receive the Holy Spirit. He joins us to the new humanity under the authority and care of Jesus Christ, the second Adam. By the power of the Spirit we undergo a fundamental internal change: we have put off the old man with his practices and have put on the new man, who is being renewed in knowledge after the image of his Creator.[23]

What the Christian finds in his everyday experience is that, on the one hand, he is a new man being renewed by the Holy Spirit. On the other hand, he discovers, sometimes to his great surprise, that the old man still lurks in the corners. It would not be so bad if the old man would lie there and play dead. But no, not only does he not lie still; he stirs up a little resistance here, and he makes a little contact with an outside enemy there. Before long, the old man — our flesh — threatens to overwhelm us.

When we recognize this plight, we have a choice: we can either decide what has to change and gather the strength of our will to do it, or we can decide that this is a problem for the Holy Spirit to handle and turn it over

[23] See Col. 3:9-10.

to Him. Which of the two would you choose? If you se-
lect the first approach, you may as well put down this
book. Many Christians have tried it and have demon-
strated conclusively that it doesn't work.

We sometimes have difficulty surrendering a problem to the power and authority of the Holy Spirit because we don't understand how to do it very well. We
don't have much experience in yielding areas of our life
to Him. I think the following story will help.

⚓

Only the Lord can subdue the flesh

Imagine that you are employed as an officer on a
magnificent ocean liner. Your life aboard ship is very
difficult. Not only is the job demanding, but, what's
worse, the captain is a cruel man. Vile and arrogant, he
acts out of caprice rather than reason. His orders always
seem completely arbitrary and counterproductive. His
regular fits of rage sometimes climax in beatings. Occasionally he adopts an excessively pleasant manner to
conceal some nasty plan.

His tyranny over the crew and passengers continues
until the owner of the company takes a cruise on the
liner. He notices the problems caused by the captain,

and he takes action that very day by firing him and putting a new captain in charge. The new captain makes quite a contrast to the old one. He is good and strong, a man everyone respects and obeys. He knows how to lead the crew, to bring things back into order, and to care for all the people on the ship.

But the old captain doesn't leave the liner, even though the owner of the company had directed him to. The old captain takes up residence in a storage room deep in the ship's hold. There, bitterly resenting his ouster, he nurses his ill feelings toward the company and the new captain. Occasionally, he strolls about the ship, menacing the crew just as he used to when he was captain. He barks orders that contradict the new captain's directions. Out of fear and a strange forgetfulness, crew members often do what he says.

On one of these strolls, the old captain struts into your office and gives you his orders for the day, just as he used to. When you start to resist, he bullies you with threats.

You are now faced with a choice. You could try to handle the situation on your own. You have always wanted to put the old captain down. You are a little bigger than he, and you suspect that you are a whole lot

stronger. You would enjoy smashing him one or some-
how taking care of the matter yourself.

Or you could bring the matter to the attention of the
new captain. You could say to the old captain, "You
must be making some mistake. I don't work for you anymore. Have you forgotten about the new captain? You'll
need to take up the matter with him. In fact, here he is
right now. Why don't you talk to him about it?" Instead
of relying on yourself, you can place the problem under the authority of the new captain, letting him deal
with the old captain and his antics.

This parallels our situation as Christians. Through
the power of Christ's death and Resurrection, we have
put off the old man with his evil ways and put on the
new man. The old captain has been fired, and we are
under the authority of the new captain. When our flesh,
behaving like the old captain, attempts to usurp its old
place of power in order to mold us according to its ways,
we face the same choice as the officer in the story. We
have the option of trying to handle our flesh on our own
or turning the matter over to the Lord, letting Him deal
with our flesh and its bag of tricks.

Many of us find the first option attractive. Our flesh
has caused us difficulty for years. Wouldn't it be fun to

muscle it into place for once? We think we're now a little bit bigger than it is. But the better and safer option is to place the problem under the authority of our new Captain.

Yielding our problems to the Holy Spirit within us requires that we change our approach. We must renounce all possibility of handling things by ourselves. We must stop trying to do the right thing on our own. We should stop demanding that God help us do things our way. We must refuse to follow the commands of our flesh. We must rely on the authority of the Lord and the power of the Spirit to resolve our problems. Our new Captain has the power to subdue our flesh.

⚜

We must make Christ our Lord

Accomplishing the switch means turning every area of our lives over to the Lord. In the story, the new captain had to take authority over life on the ocean liner in every detail. One of the first things he did when he assumed his responsibilities was to tour the entire ship, exploring every hold and stateroom, talking to crew and passengers alike. He was both assessing conditions and extending his authority over every area of the ship.

The same thing must happen for us. We must give every area of our lives over to the Lord. Our new Captain makes His exploratory tour, assessing conditions and extending His authority throughout our lives. Because everything must come under His lordship, we would be wise to throw open every nook and cranny for His attention.

If we take inventory now, however, we will probably find that we have held back some areas. An honest look at the places where our old captain — the flesh — operates will uncover more work for the Lord. When we have a problem that won't go away, an objective assessment will tell us exactly what it is we have yet to yield to Christ's authority.

Sometimes we even seal off an area, secretly hoping that the Lord will overlook it. Our new Captain approaches a closed door and gently inquires, "What's in there?" Surprised that He even noticed the door, we respond nervously, "Nothing." "Well," He continues kindly, "if it's nothing, I don't suppose you'll mind if I have a look."

As He moves again toward the door, we quickly step in front of it. "It didn't occur to me that You would ever want to go in there," we say. "Oh, but I do. You're ready for it," He replies. "I don't think I want You to see what's there," is our truthful answer.

⚜

We must resolve to overcome our problems

We may desire to follow the Lord in everything and still attempt to shut Him out of an area where we're having a problem. The following account illustrates the point further.

Leo is the owner of a small business and a leader in his parish's youth program. He is very effective at both responsibilities. He is twenty-eight, married, has one child, and has been following the Lord with conviction since he was twenty years old. But occasionally he had bouts with depression, although he never regarded it as much of a problem.

But Laura, his wife of three years, thought otherwise. She told Leo that his brief periods of sluggishness and withdrawal were difficult times for her. On those days, Leo, usually a very good husband, would renege on his responsibilities, letting her fend for herself. Because he knew that he was making life difficult for Laura, Leo made some efforts to stop getting depressed. But it was a struggle he couldn't seem to win.

As he prayed about it, he began to realize that he enjoyed getting depressed. That was the root of the problem. He wasn't able to receive the Lord's help because he liked dropping out now and then.

As soon as Leo told the Lord that he didn't want to get depressed anymore, he was finally able to overcome his bouts with depression. Instead of giving in to his flesh, which kept repeating its invitations to him to take a little vacation and withdraw, he gave the area over to the Lord.

In effect, he said to his flesh, "There must be some mistake. I don't have to obey you any longer. Have you forgotten the new Captain? Here he is right now. Why don't you ask him if he'd like to go on a little vacation and withdraw with you?"

Leo had told the Lord, "I want to change. I don't like the idea of getting depressed. I want You to deal with my flesh and set me free of this impulse." And God worked the change Leo asked for. Yielding to the Lord released him from the hold of the flesh. For the past eight years Leo has had control of the area, knowing he had it within his power to refuse to get depressed. Most of the time, with the exception of one or two slips, he has chosen well.

Take another example. Betty is a single forty-year-old woman. Like Mark, whom we met in the first chapter, she has had a problem with sexual fantasies. For many years, discipline and willpower helped Betty manage the area somewhat, but she still regarded her sexual daydreaming as a fairly serious problem.

Things got worse a few years ago after she attended a seminar on sexuality for single people. The seminar was a well-intentioned effort to help single Catholics confront their sexuality and deal with it more openly. In Betty's case, it was a disaster.

For a while afterward, she indulged her fantasies. She also began to have a problem with masturbation, something that had never been a problem for her before. One of the books recommended at the seminar suggested that single people allow themselves to become secretly infatuated with a member of the opposite sex. Betty tried it and was embarrassed about the crush she developed on a young married man in her parish.

That bit of ridiculous advice was a blessing in disguise. Betty was so revolted by her experience that she rejected the book and the seminar. She talked her problem over with a married woman who had been her friend for years. This woman suggested to Betty that she hadn't yet won her struggle with sexual fantasy and masturbation because she hadn't turned the problem area over to the Lord. Although she wanted to stop, Betty found her sexual fantasies a little too pleasant. In prayer, Betty said she wanted to change and asked the Lord to give her the self-control she needed to curb her unruly desires.

Betty has improved considerably since she began to ask the Lord to change her. Her problem with masturbation seems to be over. She still has times when disorderly sexual thoughts seem to overwhelm her. But she gives in to these thoughts less frequently and is now confident that the Lord will give her greater control in that area as well.

A key to being able to yield a problem to the Lord is simply to want to be changed in that area.

So far, we have uncovered three basic steps for overcoming persistent problems in our life. These principles (and others in subsequent chapters) will be the makings of a strategy that will help us to overcome the flesh. The first three parts in the strategy are as follows:

• We must honestly admit we have a problem.

• We must place the problem under the Lord's authority for Him to correct, setting aside our tendency to handle it on our own.

• We must want to be changed so much that we will examine our life carefully enough to root out whatever it is that we are attached to.

Chapter Seven

Expect Jesus to conquer your problems

Catholics are acquainted with several kinds of faith. First, there is the kind of faith that is expressed when people make an adult commitment to the Lord. They exercise a certain kind of faith that brings them into a personal relationship with Jesus Christ. This faith connects us with God. Through it, they appropriate the basic elements of their relationship with the Lord: Baptism, life in the Holy Spirit, membership in the Church. This is the kind of faith that makes us Christians.

Second, we use the word *faith* for the assent we give to the truths of Christianity. When our intellect submits to a doctrine of the Church or a truth of Scripture, we say we believe it. When we accept the truths declared in the Apostles' Creed — the Trinity, the Incarnation, the Redemption, the Church — we say we believe. This is doctrinal faith, and it is the guarantor of Christian orthodoxy.

We also have a third kind of faith, an underlying trust in God that can be called daily faith. This faith assures us that the Lord provides and cares for us. God sustains us in being, keeps us from harm, anticipates our needs, and knows our thoughts. We know these to be facts, and we count on them. This is the faith we live by.

These varieties of faith are all good and useful. In fact, they're essential. But they're distinct from the kind of faith we need to overcome problems rooted in the flesh. We can possess all three and yet not be able to conquer a persistent difficulty in our life.

John, for example, was a member in good standing at his parish. From the day of his Confirmation as a teenager, he had won the admiration of many parishioners. An excellent college student, he was a youth leader in his parish and taught in its religious-education program. If there were a way to test the kinds of faith present in a person, John would rate high on all three varieties described above.

John's father had abandoned his family when John was twelve. Consequently, John had a rough time of it in the next few years. As a teenager, he developed a number of emotional problems, which he took with him into adulthood, although he kept them hidden from others. He had to deal constantly with guilt feelings that had grown to mountain-high proportions. Beneath those feelings of guilt, he felt a profound self-hatred. Underneath the surface of his articulate self-confidence, John was often troubled by self-contempt. When he exercised leadership at church, he often thought of himself as a hypocrite.

One day, as John was talking over his problems with a family friend he had grown to trust, the man exclaimed, "John, you think your problems are so big — you're so proud of your sins — that you think Jesus Himself isn't big enough to help you." Although John believed in the Lord, the friend continued, he didn't really expect the Lord to do anything about his problems. In fact, John didn't believe that the Lord *could* do anything about them.

⚶

Overcoming problems requires expectant faith

John wasn't able to overcome his self-hatred because he failed to exercise the right kind of faith. Overcoming problems rooted in the flesh requires *expectant* faith. Expectant faith believes the Lord will do what must be done to set us free. This is the kind of faith David exercised in his combat with Goliath. Even as he released the polished stone from his sling, he fully expected that it would strike Goliath's unprotected forehead. He knew the Lord would act to save him.

When the Apostles urged the Lord, saying, "Increase our faith!" Jesus responded: "If you had faith the size of a mustard seed, you could say to this sycamore, 'Be uprooted and transplanted into the sea,' and it would obey you."[24] Jesus was teaching the Apostles about expectant faith.

Once, on the road to Jerusalem, Jesus cursed a fig tree that bore no fruit, and it withered on the spot. The disciples asked why this happened. Jesus replied, "Truly, I say to you, if you have faith and never doubt, you will not only do what has been done to the fig tree, but even if you say to this mountain, 'Be taken up and cast into the sea,' it will be done. And whatever you ask in prayer, you will receive, if you have faith."[25] Expectant faith begins to look for the desired change the moment the prayer is spoken.

[24]Luke 17:5-6 (New American Bible).
[25]Matt. 21:21-22.

Our problems may seem bigger than the mountain the Lord pointed to, promising that faith could cast it into the sea. They may be more deeply entrenched than the sycamore tree that faith could pluck out of the ground like a carrot. To experience release from them, however, we must be confident that God will act to deliver us. And why shouldn't we be confident? The very same Holy Spirit of Him who raised Jesus Christ from the dead is at work in us.[26]

Isn't the Lord big enough to free us from our problems? You would think that as Christians, as men and women who know and love the Lord, we would have no difficulty believing that Jesus has the power to deal with anything we come up against. After all, we have seen Him prevail in valiant combat with Satan.

In *The Great Divorce*, C. S. Lewis describes what the outskirts of Heaven might be like. In that region, one butterfly could devour all Hell with one small bite, if the Lord so allowed. That is reality. Of course Jesus is big enough to overcome all of our problems. Even delicate creatures dwelling in the foothills of His kingdom can chew up Hell itself and spit out the bones.

[26]See Rom. 8:11.

Yet we lose sight of this fact in everyday Christian life. Our problems loom up to shadowy heights, and Jesus seems dwarfed as we grope among these giants. When we read in Scripture things such as "Whatever you ask in my name, I will do it,"[27] we say, "Yes, of course that's true." But in our mind's eye we add a little footnote: "Except for me. I'm different."

⚹

We must believe that Jesus will help us

When we think this way, we're being double-minded, a malady that weakens our faith. James diagnoses our condition thus: "But let him ask in faith, with no doubting, for he who doubts is like a wave of the sea that is driven and tossed by the wind. For that person must not suppose that a double-minded man, unstable in all his ways, will receive anything from the Lord."[28]

The double-minded person opens a chasm between the truth and his problem. The truth is that Jesus is bigger than our problems. With a double mind we say, "Yes, I believe that, but I really don't think I'll ever overcome

[27]John 14:13.
[28]James 1:6-8.

this problem." The chasm is right there between the *yes* and the *but*. Only expectant faith can bridge that gap. When we exercise that kind of faith, we not only know the truth, but we also hold ourselves to it.

In his letter to the Christians at Rome, Paul acknowledges that they *know* they are no longer bound to commit sin. They have truly participated in the death of Christ. But he reminds them that it isn't enough simply to know the truth. They must also hold themselves to it: "So you also must consider yourselves dead to sin and alive to God in Christ Jesus."[29]

If we know a fact but fail to hold ourselves to it, we may contradict it by our actions. If I know that I have three thousand dollars but act as though I haven't a cent to my name, I may soon find myself starving. The same is true for the life of faith.

If the power of the Holy Spirit that courses through my life is to strengthen me and free me from the effects of the flesh, I must act according to my knowledge of God's presence and power. Expectant faith needn't be some majestic bridge over the chasm between knowing the truth and holding myself to it. My faith need be only

[29]Rom. 6:11.

a tiny key, mustard-seed-size, to unlock the channels of divine power that Jesus has already put at my disposal. Expectant faith holds me to the fact that Jesus is bigger than my problems, and He will unleash storms of His grace to conquer them.

⚜

We must persevere in expectant faith

Very often we fail to exercise expectant faith for our problems. We have tried almost everything and have had little or no success. Our discouragement over a particular problem has matured into despair. It has settled securely around the problem area and turned to stone. We can't budge it. We have lost all hope of getting free of it.

We know that something of this order has happened to us when we find ourselves saying, "Well, that's just the way I am. We're all going to have to live with it." (Someone might justifiably respond, "What do you mean *we?* Maybe you have decided to live with it, friend, but that doesn't mean I have.")

As we take stock of our lives, we may very well find one or two problems that resist change, no matter how much faith we muster. These are areas in which we may have to fight for the faith to see them corrected.

In Tolkien's *The Lord of the Rings*, Gandalf faces off against a mighty, evil creature, a Balrog, on the bridge at Khazad Dum. The wizard declares to the Balrog that by virtue of the authority bestowed on Gandalf, it cannot pass. Gandalf destroys the bridge, casting the flaming beast into the pit, but with a whisk of its tail, the Balrog drags the wizard with him. Gandalf is locked in conflict with this fiery beast in the bowels of the earth. He endures the white heat of the fire and is dragged up endless stairs to a mountaintop, where he finally conquers this servant of the enemy.

Gandalf had to fight for faith. He was a steward of the affairs of Middle Earth, charged with its defense against the gathering storm. Yet darkness had reached out to claim him. He hung on and fought until, at the last moment, an eagle rescued him from death itself.

Christians facing difficult problems must imitate this brand of "fight." Doggedness is a common companion to expectant faith. Nothing should daunt us, be it temptation, fire, darkness, or height. If we are tempted to give in, we must fight to hold on to faith.

If Gandalf seems too far removed from reality, take the Lord Himself for your model. The Lord expected His Father to restore Him to life. Jesus attained the glory of the Resurrection only by fighting through His Crucifixion and death. He had to fight for faith, even though He knew the Father's plan. You may try to dismiss this by saying that Jesus was God. But He was also a man, one like us, who had weaknesses, fears, and doubts.[30] In the face of death, the man Jesus fought for faith. He won His battle in the garden on the eve of His death. His winning makes our fighting easier and our victory assured.

Contrary to the way it might seem at first, fighting for faith is not a lapse into willpower Christianity. By definition, willpower Christianity leaves faith out. It works not by faith, but by self-reliance. Fighting for faith is the alternative, both to giving up on the problem and to making one last attempt to handle it ourselves. Fighting through will keep us in touch with the only power that can save us.

Fifteen years ago John began to believe that Jesus Christ was bigger than his self-contempt. Now, as a result of expecting the Lord to change him, his problem with self-hatred is only a memory. If he has any problem in that area now, it may be one of overconfidence.

[30]See Heb. 4:14-15, 5:7-8.

Jesus is big enough. Are we ready to expect Him to release us from our problems?

We can now add the fourth step to our strategy for overcoming the flesh:

- We must expect the Lord to change us. It isn't enough to know that Jesus is bigger than our problems. We must hold ourselves to that truth, even to the point of fighting to lay hold of it.

Chapter Eight

⚘

Express joy and give thanks
even in your problems

＊

Taking stock of our problems has its drawbacks. As we compute the number of things that are wrong in our lives, we may be staggered by the sum. Reading books (such as this one) that offer to help us overcome our problems may even increase our difficulties before they bring relief. We may learn, for example, that some qualities we regarded as virtues are actually vices. We may discover that areas we never paid much attention to are actually traps from which we should get free. In short, tallying up our problems may only focus us on the problems themselves.

At times, one or another of our more persistent problems may stir up so much turmoil that we can think of almost nothing else. For example, anxiety and suppressed anger can so agitate us that they absorb all of our mental energy. Or we may become so preoccupied with some personality defect that we spend all our time worrying about how to change. We might even locate the nexus of all our problems in some act of habitual wrongdoing, such as drunkenness, and become determined to quit drinking.

Nothing is wrong with trying to get free of our problems. But taking stock of our problems can fix our eyes on ourselves to a degree that is spiritually unhealthy. Self-concern prevents us from getting free of the very problems that generate it. Focusing our attention on the problems disconnects us from the power of the Holy Spirit, our only real hope for release from their grip.

⚜

We must always rejoice and give thanks

But how, in practical terms, can we turn away from our problems and turn toward the Lord for help? The most effective approach is based on the New Testament principle of rejoicing and giving thanks to the Lord in all circumstances. "Rejoice always, pray constantly, give thanks in all circumstances."[31] Joy and thankfulness are not unpredictable emotions but qualities that underlie the Christian life. We should be joyful and thankful not

[31] 1 Thess. 5:16-18.

only in good times, when we feel happy or grateful, but in bad times as well.

In the culture of the New Testament, to rejoice meant primarily to engage in the activities of celebration: singing, dancing, feasting, and so on. A person could rejoice whether he felt happy or not. Some of those neighbors dragged in to rejoice with the woman who found the coin she had lost might not have felt like partying that day.[32] The point is plain. We can rejoice even in painful circumstances without having to feel happy about them. The command is to be joyful always.

We are to give thanks in all circumstances. According to Paul, thankfulness is the proper response to every circumstance, whether good or bad. He didn't say, "Rejoice sometimes, pray occasionally, give thanks in most circumstances."

To rejoice and give thanks in the midst of our problems isn't to say that these problems are good. Problems are not good, but evil. We have every reason for wanting to be free of them. Why, then, does the New Testament teach us to rejoice in the face of difficulties?

[32] See Luke 15:8-9.

Although our difficulties aren't good in themselves, they can lead to something good. "Count it all joy, my brethren," counsels James, "when you meet various trials, for you know that the testing of your faith produces steadfastness. And let steadfastness have its full effect, that you may be perfect and complete, lacking in nothing."[33]

We are to be glad for trials because every time we pass through them, we will become more like our Father, who is perfect and complete.

The New Testament teaches us to approach our problems in a way that maintains our connection to the power of God. "We know that in everything God works for good with those who love Him, who are called according to His purpose."[34] In good and bad, virtue and vice, righteousness and wrongdoing, God works.

It isn't that we should sin in order to see grace abound.[35] Rather, our problems are reasons for rejoicing and giving thanks because they are opportunities for us to see the power of God at work in our lives.

[33]James 1:2-4.
[34]Rom. 8:28.
[35]See Rom. 6:1-2.

✳

*Thanking God in trials doesn't
require feeling good*

Once we grasp this truth, we must act on it. When we're suffering from a problem, we must thank the Lord for working it to our good. But be forewarned: we will hardly ever feel like thanking God during these times. Fortunately, the New Testament doesn't require us to feel good about our trials and difficulties, but to rejoice in the good that the Lord will work through them. We too readily equate rejoicing with feeling happy, which, although related, are not identical. Most of our problems involve a certain amount of mental or physical pain. In the midst of our anguish, we should thank God for the chance to see Him at work. We should express our eagerness to behold the change He will accomplish in us as a consequence.

The following account illustrates how this principle works.

Tony is a member of the personnel department in a software company. He and his wife, Jean, have five children under ten years of age, a fact related to his problem. He and Jean are both faithful Catholics. After the birth of their fourth child, they began using natural family planning. When Jean became pregnant with child number five, she and Tony were very surprised, to put it mildly. Motherly tenderness soon softened Jean's fears and her sense of inadequacy. She was delighted with the thought of a new baby, but knew that Tony wasn't at all happy about it.

Tony has never been known for controlling his temper. His Christian behavior has been marred occasionally by angry outbursts or by quiet, but intense, periods of slow burn. The surprise pregnancy put him in a state that ran the entire gamut of anger's possibilities. At first he was livid. Even though he stopped having outbursts, his rage simmered within and became mixed with a deep discouragement. For a month he was profoundly out of sorts, which contributed to other problems. For example, he misinterpreted the behavior of his supervisor at work, complaining bitterly and unfairly about his boss to Jean and others. His constant, suppressed fury drained and exhausted him.

When Tony's anger showed no signs of going away, his close friend Joe confronted him about it. For several years, Tony and Joe had met for lunch once a week to talk about their lives and to pray for their families. When the bout of temper struck, Tony started missing the lunch dates. Joe cornered him one day, and the two friends spent several hours talking. After hearing Tony out, Joe advised him to thank the Lord every time discouragement or anger smoldered in his heart. "That's easy for you to say," snarled Tony. "Your wife isn't pregnant." But after he had thought about Joe's words and recognized the wisdom in them, Tony began to follow his advice.

For the next month, many times a day, Tony simply thanked the Lord. At first he did it with great difficulty. It didn't seem to make a difference. He still felt miserable, angry, and discouraged. "I'm very angry, Lord," he would say, "but I'm grateful to You for all that You're doing in me. Please help Jean, for I think I'm causing her a lot of pain." It wasn't long before the thanksgiving came more easily. Before the month was over, his anger had subsided. He repented to Jean for his bad behavior. Soon Tony himself began to look forward to the birth of the baby. Tony says that ever since then, he has handled his anger more effectively. He still has to be wary, but he has more control.

Expressing thankfulness in the face of a problem opens a channel for the Lord's power to flow where it would otherwise remain blocked by self-concern. If we remain focused on the problem, we are stuck and may get hurt. The moment we turn our minds actively to the Lord, we place ourselves in a position to receive God's help and to be strengthened in the process.

ॐ

Accepting crosses can free us from the flesh

Sometimes, people deal with problems by accepting them as crosses. This may be precisely the approach the Lord wants us to take. If so, an attitude of rejoicing and thanksgiving won't make the problem go away, but it will give us the right disposition toward God.

We shouldn't think that crosses in themselves are good. The Cross of Christ was purely evil, the nexus of all that is sinful and opposed to God. Satan used it to try to obliterate the Lord. If we accept some problem as a cross, we should understand that the problem isn't itself something good. At the same time, we know that the Father brought unfathomable good from the Cross of His Son and wills to bring good out of our suffering. Accepting something as a cross, then, means acknowledging that a problem is an evil through which the Lord is working for our benefit. It is another opportunity for grace to conquer the hold of the flesh on us.

Joy and thanks in all circumstances is the fifth part of our strategy for getting free from persistent problems. We can state it thus:

• We must express joy and thanks to the Lord in our problems. Joy and thankfulness transform our problems into opportunities for the Lord to work in our lives. They turn our minds from our problems to Him.

Chapter Nine

૪

Let go of grudges

✻

A young French schoolboy watched as two Englishmen disembarked from their ship at the port of Calais. Before they knew what hit them, the lad charged at them, pushing them off the pier into the water. Not too pleased at this inhospitable gesture, the men climbed out and accosted the boy. "Just what are you trying to do? Is that any way to greet visitors to your country? A good spanking might teach you some manners. Why did you do such a thing?" The boy spat back, "That's for burning Joan of Arc at the stake!" "But that happened five hundred years ago," was the astonished response. "Yeah, but I just learned about it this morning," he replied.

Nationality jokes are banned at my house (I'm not allowed to tell them). As instruction in a certain dangerous human weakness, however, such humor does have redeeming value. Like the boy in the anecdote, people tend to hold grudges against one another for a long time. Individuals may nurse bitter memories of past rivalries for years. Nations may do it for centuries. In any case, resentment is an unhealthy practice and detrimental to all involved.

Nursing grudges is a serious stumbling block in the Christian life. Constantly recalling people's offenses and thinking of ways to pay them back creates a steady drain on our spiritual energy. Bitterness prevents us from receiving the Lord's power. It blocks our release from the problems that afflict us.

Only rarely do we succeed in damaging an offender more than we damage ourselves. The harder we try to get back at someone, the more we get hurt. As our mind reaches out in search of revenge, bitterness reaches into us, plunging its massive, expanding tentacle deep within us. Daydreams of getting even devour our time during the day. At night we lose sleep to our hurt feelings. Resentment is a spiritual tapeworm that nourishes itself at our expense. Too often we are willing to feed this parasite.

Revenge can seem so reasonable. It doesn't take much to persuade us that we have good cause to strike back. Four-year-old Mary runs in tears to her father with the complaint, "Daddy, Daddy, Tommy hit me for no reason." Five-year-old Tommy is next on the scene, explaining to his dad that the reason he hit Mary was that she hit him first. Like the children in this all-too-familiar scene, we often have good reasons for striking back at people who have mistreated us. Many times we are perfectly right. In accordance with principles of strict justice, people who wrong us ought to repent and make amends for the damage they have done.

⁂

God calls us to show mercy to others

Although this approach makes sense on one level, it can be fatal to us on another. If it's reasonable to hold others to a standard of strict justice, it's equally reasonable to hold ourselves to the same standard. Had the Lord demanded payment for the debt we piled up because of our sins, it would have cost each of us our lives. Death would have been only fair punishment for us. What else could we expect?

The Lord, however, dealt with us according to a different standard, a standard of mercy. He was not put off by our sin. In the face of an endless inventory of wrongdoing and direct offenses against His Person, He sent His Son to an ignominious death to cancel our debt to Him.

"While we were still weak, at the right time Christ died for the ungodly. Why, one will hardly die for a righteous man — though perhaps for a good man one will dare even to die. But God shows His love for us in that while we were yet sinners Christ died for us."[36] Instead of exacting what we owed Him, the Lord forgave us. Paul says that the Lord "canceled the bond which stood against us with its legal demands; this He set aside, nailing it to the Cross."[37]

If we want the Lord to release us from our wrongdoing, we must release others from the wrongs they have done to us. This is what we pray in the Lord's Prayer. Instructed by Jesus Himself, we ask the Father to bestow the same measure of forgiveness on us as we bestow on others. If we have been stingy with our forgiveness until now, we had best hasten to become more generous. We ought to understand the consequences of praying the Lord's Prayer. We don't want to commit ourselves to a limited measure of forgiveness and mercy each time we say, "And forgive us our trespasses as we forgive those who trespass against us."

[36]Rom. 5:6-8.
[37]Col. 2:14.

If we are harboring resentment, grudges, or bitterness against others, the New Testament commands us to put them away. "Let all bitterness and wrath and anger and clamor and slander be put away from you, with all malice, and be kind to one another, tenderhearted, forgiving one another, as God in Christ forgave you."[38]

When we hold a grudge, we are holding a claim against someone. We write out spiritual IOUs. We keep strict accounts, planning to exact the very last penny. In our ledger, we hold IOUs against our parents (for quarreling between themselves and manipulating us); against brothers and sisters (for belittling us and getting more parental attention, or so it seemed); against spouses (for some petty fault or slip of the tongue); against children (for lack of respect and for turning out different than we had planned). We hold IOUs against friends, neighbors, coworkers, acquaintances, and so on. If we are to experience freedom ourselves, we must cancel all these debts. We must deal with our IOUs the way God dealt with ours: He "canceled the bond which stood against us with its legal demands; this He set aside, nailing it to the Cross."

[38]Eph. 4:31.

⚖

Tearing up spiritual IOUs
helps rid us of resentment

There is a practical way to get rid of resentment. Make a list of all those people toward whom you have resentments. Begin with the people closest to you — parents, spouses, brothers, sisters, and children — and move outward from there. You might want to list each on a separate slip of paper. Then tear up the IOUs one by one. Forgive each of them, no matter what they have done to offend you.

You may come up against one or two IOUs that you feel you just can't tear up, because the hurt was too big.

A common mistake is to think that forgiveness is something a person *feels* rather than something a person *does*. If we wait until we feel like forgiving, we'll probably take others' IOUs with us to the grave. It helps to feel like forgiving someone we must forgive, but if we don't feel like it, we should go ahead and forgive anyway. Once we have torn up the IOUs, once we have stopped dwelling on the offense against us, our feelings toward the person will improve. Through the power of forgiveness, many a person has ended up liking someone they thought they would always hate.

Tearing up IOUs is usually a unilateral action. For our part, we release people who have offended us. We say by our action that we no longer intend to collect whatever we think they owe us. Tearing up IOUs doesn't mean saying to each person toward whom we feel resentful, "I forgive you for the time you did this" or, "I don't hold that against you anymore." Usually putting aside resentments and bitterness is something I do privately, between the Lord and me. But doing so can suggest ways of straightening out broken relationships. We should be open to taking further steps if they seem right. Talking over with someone we trust what we think we must do may help us act prudently in mending relationships.

The Lord gives us the grace to forgive and forgive generously. We should begin now by tearing up the IOUs we are holding, and we should repeat the process regularly.

We can now add a sixth part to our strategy for getting free from the influence of the flesh:

> • We must put aside all resentment, bitterness, and grudges. These are obstacles to our spiritual freedom that prevent us from experiencing the power of the Lord in our lives.

Chapter Ten

❧

Control your thoughts

There is an old saying that goes something like this: "Although many birds may fly around your head, you don't have to let them nest in your hair." There's a kernel of wisdom to this saying that we would do well to take seriously. Innumerable thoughts pass through our minds every day, each one clamoring for attention and looking for a place to settle in. If we welcome them all, we'll be in trouble. We must be very selective about those we choose to make our own.

Our thoughts significantly influence our actions. It's a mistake to believe that even passing thoughts have no effect on us. That is simply not true. Each human being is an integrated whole, not a collection of independent units. What we see and touch affects our thinking. What we think and imagine affects our behavior.

If we are to make any progress in overcoming the flesh, we must be concerned for our minds. Remember, the flesh works in our intellect. That may even be the main way it works in our lives. As we have seen, Jesus taught that evil thoughts corrupt us. "But what comes out of the mouth proceeds from the heart, and this defiles a man. For out of the heart come evil thoughts, murder, adultery, fornication, theft, false witness, slander."[39] Wrongdoing doesn't just happen. It's the fruit of wicked contemplation.

When we put on the new man and put off the old, we are given a new mind. Paul says, "Be renewed in the spirit of your minds, and put on the new nature [the new man], created after the likeness of God in true righteousness and holiness."[40] The new man has the mind of Christ, a mind that directs us in good behavior. But the old man, you'll recall, doesn't slink off and disappear as he ought. He lingers, putting his thoughts into our heads. The mind of the new man works like a finely tuned gyroscope, governing our behavior from within, under the influence of the Holy Spirit. But the mind of the old man operates like radar, locating the attractive, but dangerous, influences of the world outside.

[39]Matt. 15:18-19.
[40]Eph. 4:23.

Since more voices than just our own speak in our thoughts, we shouldn't automatically assume that what we think is what we are. We're not responsible for every thought that flits through our minds. The flesh is behind some of them, and we can be sure it isn't trying to influence us for the good.

⚜

Temptations themselves aren't sinful

A major way in which the flesh attacks our minds is by welcoming the Devil's temptations. Now, temptations don't tell us much, if anything, about the person receiving them. They tell us more about the one sending them. They reveal the strategy the enemy has chosen to ensnare this son or daughter of God. They expose the enemy's nature rather than any reality about his prey.

We tend to think that temptation is sin, or at least so close to being sin that it isn't worth the effort to resist it. Now, if that thought doesn't come from the flesh, it comes from the Devil himself. A temptation that passes through our mind is no different in itself from any other thought. We can decide how we will interpret it and whether we will embrace it. Temptations are dangerous only if we let them take root in our mind. If we keep our distance from them and replace them with other, nobler thoughts, we have dealt with them correctly.

The flesh works on our minds in numerous other ways. It lies to us, deceiving us into thinking we must sin. The flesh persuades us that we will never be free from this or that problem. The old man brings his cronies home with him, giving them the run of our minds, as if he, and not the Lord, owned the place. At his invitation, discouragement comes in and works us over. Then his companion, despair, takes his turn whipping us.

The flesh supplies a spiritual calculator to help us measure our thoughts and actions according to the standards of our friends and the standards of our secular Western culture. Our flesh also attempts to define our self-image for us: it would have us believe that we're merely worthless, guilty humans, doomed to be fodder for Satan. If it can get us to feel bad about ourselves, we'll be easier to push around.

⚜

*Our mind requires proper
care and nourishment*

What goes on in our minds, then, has a lot to do with the degree of Christian freedom that we experience.

Dwelling on evil thoughts constricts our freedom. Yielding our minds to the Holy Spirit expands it. "For those who live according to the flesh set their minds on the things of the flesh, but those who live according to the Spirit set their minds on the things of the Spirit. To set the mind on the flesh is death, but to set the mind on the Spirit is life and peace. For the mind that is set on the flesh is hostile to God; it does not submit to God's law; indeed it cannot; and those who are in the flesh cannot please God."[41]

Whom do we want to win the battle for our mind: the flesh or the Holy Spirit? If we want the Holy Spirit to prevail, we'll need to take an active, rather than a passive, approach. Unless we actively present our minds to the Lord, we'll allow our thoughts to welcome among them the voices of evil spirits. Taking active concern for our minds involves both refusing the influence of the flesh and yielding to the grace of the Spirit.

We should regard our minds as a battleground over which the Lord has already prevailed. We need only guard the battleground to prevent the old man from moving his troops back into position. The Lord has

[41]Rom. 8:5-8.

captured the territory and commissioned us as His lieu-tenants to hold it in His name. But the enemy would desperately like to reclaim it.

Our strategy should be to use the Lord's authority, backed up by His power, to marshal our thoughts. We are fully equipped to keep the flesh from dictating our thoughts and from infiltrating our minds with ideas that come from the enemy. Our job is to refuse to give evil thoughts any place in our minds. We must be diligent about rejecting invitations to sin. We must distance our minds from the parade of negative thoughts competing for attention.

Computer programmers have an expression that applies to our minds as well: "Garbage in, garbage out." If the computer generates a jumble of confused material, we can be sure that the source of the problem can be located in what was put into the computer. The same is true for our minds. If they produce evil thoughts that culminate in wicked behavior, we can be sure that one source of the problem has to do with what was put into our minds. Garbage in, garbage out.

Taking an active concern to protect our minds means being wary about what we take in. The media, as a cursory review indicates, are increasingly anti-Christian in content. Sensible Christians won't pretend that they can view or read just anything without adverse effects. We must control our reading and viewing carefully.

The action we take to protect our minds isn't merely the negative action of refusing evil thoughts. We must also yield our minds to the Holy Spirit. When we put on the new man, we put on the mind of Christ. Paul says that our new man "is being renewed in knowledge after the image of its Creator."[42] The Holy Spirit activates the mind of Christ in us. He helps us understand the Lord's ways. He confers the practical wisdom we need to apply the teachings of the Church and of Scripture in our daily lives. The Holy Spirit empowers us to resist the evil thoughts of the old man. He implants in us thoughts that bear fruit in righteous behavior.

Yielding our minds to the Holy Spirit means submitting them to the Lord's authority. Paul says that the mind set on the flesh does not, and cannot, submit to God's law. Conversely, the mind set on the Spirit is a mind that submits itself to God's law. Living by the Spirit means believing without question what the Lord says and obeying Him.

[42]Col. 3:10.

If we want the Spirit to inspire and form our thoughts, we must give Him something to work with. We aren't supposed to still our minds to the point of blankness. Scripture tells us, not to eliminate all thought in order to await passively some distant voice, but rather to fill our minds with good and true thoughts. "Whatever is true, whatever is honorable, whatever is just, whatever is pure, whatever is lovely, whatever is gracious, if there is any excellence, if there is anything worthy of praise, think about these things."[43]

We should all read Scripture daily, setting aside at least fifteen minutes to fill our minds with inspired thoughts. We should also read sound Catholic books and make use of other Christian media. If we fill our minds with excellent materials, we can expect them to produce excellent thoughts that lead to holiness.

Taking an active approach to protect our minds is part of our strategy to attain Christian freedom.

• We must guard our thoughts, refusing to let the flesh influence our minds, and yielding our minds instead to the Holy Spirit.

[43]Phil. 4:8.

Chapter Eleven

Seek committed Christian
relationships

Nineteenth-century socialists believed that the human environment was the source of the evil that human beings experience. They alleged that economic, social, and political laws generated problems for people. Karl Marx, for example, believed that class struggle was an economic law that chained humanity in misery.

Early socialists held that the way to eliminate the influence of evil on man, the way to resolve human problems, was to place humans in the right environment. Some of them constructed model human communities designed either for agrarian or industrial settings. In controlled situations, where liberty, equality, and fraternity were to operate untrammeled by greed and other wickedness, human beings would excel and prosper. So they reasoned.

Planned communities, with carefully designed buildings and grounds and craftily conceived approaches to relationships, work, and survival were attempted in England and America. For the most part, these planned human environments were dismal failures. People didn't behave any better in them than in other environments.

Nineteenth-century socialist theory was built on a certain naïveté about the human condition. Socialists simply didn't believe that human beings were innately flawed. Removed from ordinary society in which economic laws, for example, played havoc with them, and placed in an ideal, planned community, people were supposed to progress to perfection.

This view didn't adequately reckon with what human beings are up against. These social engineers were like people who would construct a beautifully designed wooden platform over the mouth of an active volcano. What kind of security could such a platform provide? These social engineers didn't reckon with the world, sin, or the Devil. Many early socialists, in fact, were materialists who scoffed at the idea of any kind of spiritual world, to say nothing of the existence of personal evil spirits.

The fatal weakness of their schemes was that they failed to acknowledge that humanity is flawed. Human beings are good, but they have evil tendencies that come from the flesh. When people are placed in a carefully planned social environment, they may behave in a good way or a bad way. The environment may have an effect on them, but it isn't the only thing that determines their behavior. The ordinary social environment may be evil because some factors are at work in it to cause problems bigger than the individuals can control. The work of the flesh in us only contributes to those problems. But moving to a planned community doesn't deal with the real source of the problems.

⚜

Christian community is part of a healthy environment

For all this, there is a kernel of truth in the idea of building healthy human environments. This is precisely what the Lord intended the new humanity to be. Through the work of Christ and the work of the Holy Spirit, mankind was released from the grip of its ancient enemies. Jesus, the second Adam, founded a new race of men and women. They were to live their lives fully for God and in union with one another. This new humanity is the Church, and its life is to be lived out in Christian community.

Christian community isn't something that just happens. Christians must build it in the midst of ordinary society. For that to happen, individuals must be brought to an adult commitment to the Lord and into committed relationships with one another.

Not all parishes or Catholic groups are Christian communities in this sense. Of course, all are part of the Christian community that is the entire new humanity, but local Christian community is something that we must work at: by developing committed relationships; learning how to care for one another; growing in the freedom to share our whole life with others. None of these comes naturally. The flesh does its best to confound our efforts to attain the important elements of community life.

Healthy relationships help free us from problems

Christians who are involved in parishes or groups that have built an environment of committed personal relationships seem to have an easier time overcoming the flesh. For many, some kinds of problems seem to go away as a result of living in a Christian environment.

Other problems are resolved more slowly but become easier to deal with and correct.

Why should committed Christian personal relationships have so great an effect on us? Precisely because many of our personal problems are rooted in twisted personal relationships. Participation in a parish that has healthy relationships can provide the impetus that frees a person from problems that originated in wrong ways of relating. Consider the following examples.

Jim was a man riddled with fear. It controlled him to the point that he had become emotionally disturbed. He would, at times, be so immobilized by anxiety that he would skip work for a week, isolating himself in his room. Jim tried every conceivable spiritual device to free himself, but found no help until he became an active participant in a small group in his parish. Jim and his pastor attribute his freedom from fear to the fact that for the last five years he has been in regular contact with men and women who love and care for him.

Kathy, who had a problem with suppressed anger and shyness, discovered that she changed significantly when she became associated with a prayer group in her parish. After seven years with that group, she no longer has a problem with suppressed anger. She has overcome shyness enough to take her turn at leading the group's meetings. Kathy recognizes that the foundation of her problem with anger and shyness was built by a long history of bad relationships with her family and friends. Her anger stemmed from her frustration over not being able to deal with the negativity and criticalness that characterized her daily contacts. Shyness protected her from these difficulties. Simple, straightforward relating in the prayer group removed the root of her frustration. The encouragement of others has been a major factor for healing her shyness.

John, who began to get free of self-hatred when he decided Jesus was big enough, also says that participating faithfully in a parish prayer group was an important part of his healing. In particular, regular work alongside other Catholic men and women who respected him and expressed affection for him made a big difference for his self-image.

Sound Christian relationships can free us from the flesh because they orient us toward the Lord and toward serving others. "Do nothing from selfishness or conceit," Paul instructed the Philippians, "but in humility count others better than yourselves. Let each of you look not only to his own interests, but also to the interests of others."[44] Selfishness and conceit are problems that stem from the flesh. Paul's antidote for both is to occupy ourselves totally in serving others. The flesh wants us to keep our eyes on ourselves. It encourages us to focus on our problems. Deliverance from selfishness, conceit, and other problems comes when we take our eyes off ourselves and our problems and begin to meet the needs of others. Once our inward stare is broken, we can more freely turn to the Lord, the only One who can release us from our difficulties.

Now we can fit the last part of the strategy into place. Committed Christian personal relationships are in themselves an important source of freedom from the grip of the flesh. They turn us to the Lord and to others, providing opportunities for us to appropriate the freedom we've already received. This yields the final practical step:

• We must seek committed Christian personal relationships that are a source of freedom from the grip of the flesh.

[44]Phil. 2:3-4.

Chapter Twelve

*Let the Lord
change you*

⚘

We have developed a practical strategy for overcoming the grip of the flesh in our lives. Now we can gather together all of the parts to get a comprehensive view of the approach:

- We must honestly admit we have a problem.

- We must place our problem under the Lord's authority for Him to correct, setting aside our tendency to try to handle it on our own.

- We must want to be changed so much that we will examine our life carefully enough to root out whatever it is that we are attached to.

- We must expect the Lord to change us. It isn't enough to know that Jesus is bigger than our problems; we must hold ourselves to that truth, even to the point of fighting to lay hold of it.

• We must express joy and thanks to the Lord in our problems. Joy and thanksgiving transform our problems into opportunities for the Lord to work in our lives. They turn our minds from our problems to Him.

• We must put aside all resentment, bitterness, and grudges. These are obstacles to our spiritual freedom that prevent us from experiencing the power of the Lord in our lives.

• We must guard our thoughts, refusing to let the flesh influence our minds, and yielding our minds instead to the Holy Spirit.

• We must seek committed Christian personal relationships that are a source of freedom from the grip of the flesh.

There is some risk in setting forth the strategy in this form. It tempts us to begin with a set of rules instead of with the Holy Spirit. If this set of principles subtly seduces us into taking a willpower approach, we will have fallen victim to the old man all over again.

We should approach the strategy, not merely as a list of things to do, but as an orientation for our lives, one that places us in a position to receive power from the Lord.

Remember, we can't free ourselves from the grip of the flesh on our own. Most of the work that must be done to release us from our problems is God's work, not ours. Christ has defeated Satan, sin, and death. The Holy Spirit masters our flesh. Our part is to cooperate with His grace.

If we work too hard to get free, our attention once again will focus on the problem. When we cry out with the Christian in Romans, "Wretched man that I am! Who will deliver me from this body of death?" we won't answer, "I will." Or will we?

No, only the Lord can free us. Let us present ourselves to Him so that He can release us from the grip of problems that we can't overcome.

Biographical Note

Bert Ghezzi

Bert Ghezzi was born in Pittsburgh, Pennsylvania. After graduating from Duquesne University with a bachelor of arts in history and classics, he earned a doctorate in history from the University of Notre Dame.

While attending Notre Dame, he married Mary Lou Cuddyre. The two became pioneers of the Catholic Charismatic Renewal movement. Bert served as a leader in that movement for many years, notably as chairman of the National Service Committee. From 1975 to 1984, he was editor of *New Covenant*, the magazine of the Charismatic Renewal. *Build With the Lord*, his first book, was the manual that gave pastoral guidance to prayer groups all over the world.

For seven years, Bert was an associate professor of history at Grand Valley State University, near Grand Rapids, Michigan. In 1974, he became editorial director for Servant Publications, which publishes popular books to help Catholics and other Christians apply the gospel to their lives and experience spiritual renewal. He later served as editorial director for Strang Communications and for the international management consulting firm Philip Crosby Associates. In 1994, he returned to Servant Publications as its editorial vice president and editorial director, positions he still holds today.

Bert is the author of thirteen books — mostly about family, spirituality, and faith — including *Voices of the Saints*, *Being Catholic Today*, and *Keeping Your Kids Catholic*. He has written for numerous magazines, including *New Covenant*, *Our Sunday Visitor*, *Christianity Today*, *Christian Retailing*, and *Catholic Digest*, and is a regular columnist for *Catholic Parent* magazine.

A member of the Fellowship of Catholic Scholars and the Academy of Christian Editors, Bert is also a sought-after inspirational speaker. Over the past thirty years, he has spoken at hundreds of meetings and conferences across the country.

Bert and Mary Lou Ghezzi have seven grown children and live in Winter Park, Florida, where they are active members of St. Mary Magdalen parish.

Sophia Institute Press®

Sophia Institute™ is a nonprofit institution that seeks to restore man's knowledge of eternal truth, including man's knowledge of his own nature, his relation to other persons, and his relation to God. Sophia Institute Press® serves this end in numerous ways: it publishes translations of foreign works to make them accessible for the first time to English-speaking readers; it brings out-of-print books back into print; and it publishes important new books that fulfill the ideals of Sophia Institute™. These books afford readers a rich source of the enduring wisdom of mankind.

Sophia Institute Press® makes these high-quality books available to the general public by using advanced technology and by soliciting donations to subsidize its general publishing costs. Your generosity can help Sophia Institute Press® to provide the public with editions of works containing the enduring wisdom of the ages.

Please send your tax-deductible contribution to the address below. We also welcome your questions, comments, and suggestions.

For your free catalog, call:
Toll-free: 1-800-888-9344

or write:
Sophia Institute Press®
Box 5284
Manchester, NH 03108

or visit our website:
www.sophiainstitute.com

Sophia Institute™ is a tax-exempt institution
as defined by the Internal Revenue Code,
Section 501(c)(3). Tax I.D. 22-2548708.